Hostile Witness

Garin Cycholl

BlazeVOX [books]

Buffalo, New York

Hostile Witness by Garin Cycholl
Copyright © 2009

Published by BlazeVOX [books]

All rights reserved. No part of this book may be
reproduced without the publisher's written permission,
except for brief quotations in reviews.

Printed in the United States of America

Book design by Geoffrey Gatza

First Edition
ISBN: 9781935402428
Library of Congress Control Number 2009925618

Thanks to Irene Siegel for the use of the cover
photograph, 'Hugged Tree, I've Been Marked for Life.'

Portions of this poem were previously included with
PFS Post Avant.

BlazeVOX [books]
14 Tremaine Ave
Kenmore, NY 14217

Editor@blazevox.org

publisher of weird little books

BlazeVOX [books]

blazevox.org

2   4   6   8   0   9   7   5   3   1

B			X

FOR CLAYTON ESHLEMAN AND MATT SVALINA

Hostile Witness

"born for opposition" and

    "eye deep in hell"—

sweet Addison muse,

    your metallic skin
sprung

        backwards into Grace,
Byron,

        Monticello

(mold is the earth's crust)

Hostile Witness

The road between them
          an America severed or
ventilated, under a hood   gasoline
bleeding soil   not *in a*
solitary palm, but in headlights

prairie

awakened in the middle of America, the
road north to Chicago, stars turning the
one A.M.—it's never just "night" you
travel through   the radio jazz as
reclusive as Detroit

                    you piss in a ditch
north of Normal—it's a joke, right? "after
the rain and the sandalwood ashes growing
cold in the braziers—the dispatches
announcing to us the collapse of the last
enemy troops—it had seemed to us the
sum of all wonder"   three men in a Chevy

moving against night anticipating some
great future violence (maybe not so
distant now, they tell
themselves) metal
against metal tires
eating asphalt voices
rubbing air   sound's
an edge against
it we

brought our guns to the hanging
our maps to the drowning our
personal defibrillators to the
campaign chicken dinner still

however great its merchandise,

the port is a haven, a repose, a
measurer of passing things

the map in the glovebox
the foxglove in the ditch
the ditch in America
America in the map   everything's
been pushed out by highway by
America by South by
West   you're traveling
one of the national roads, headed
West, when you realize Joe
McCarney is softly whistling Dixie
in the seat behind you and you're
lost here   you're headed South
towards some third-rate American
city, another one tired of history,
tired of ditches, tired of highway
but the car keeps moving and you
seem to be slowly speeding into
the map, accelerating into the curve
that turns you from Phoenix into
Birmingham, tired of all this fucking
landscape and your passenger softly
whistling to himself—"get your kicks,"
now solitary or to you, the Chevy
won't tell and neither will the foxglove
passing into North, the AM radio busted,
its music gone out somewhere south of
Joliet   *the polis in perpetual repair*

66, the Route to "permanent boomtown"
or the West, where you can "rot without
feeling it" (Los Angeles as the "end of
the road") but you're far from dead, the
night full of a "rich regenerative violence"

"a country there was, but whether land or
water, whether it was inhabited by men
or beasts, or both or neither, they knew not"

all they knew was highway—*foal-eyed &*
rubbery, they looped "the Mother Road"
or followed a crack in the nation's con-
sciousness, west by south

                    Springfield to
      Chicago and back

                  displacement

occurring throughout

(16 July 1947, the great cave of Stadium—*its burn of them*

smoke gets in your eye—"you
began to wonder if the whole
damn country wasn't infected
with moral corruption"

nothing but the geography
of the road, of the punch thrown—
referee Johnny Behr moving tirelessly,
hands to thighs, then up and circling; he
breaks them, calls them to fight

three title fights in 21 months:

>9/27/46—Zale KO's Graziano, 6 rounds (New York)
>7/16/47—Graziano TKO's Zale, 6 rounds (Chicago)
>6/10/48—Zale KO's Graziano, 3 rounds (New Jersey)

postwar kettles of blood, stirred by
light and soldier's voices—the punch
delivered after a long night of driving

four men from Springfield traveling
to Chicago for the '47 fight—Tony Zale
(159 lbs.; b. Gary, IN 1913) "the Man
of Steel"—July 16th (two years to the
day they'd opened the atom at Trinity)
18,546 filled the Chicago Stadium, its
heat "underground and intense"

(through five rounds)

my rite must yield
(the bell) Zale's fists
draw circles, lines draw
blood circling the square
of ring—men's lights and
shouts crying down out
of heaven
                    does he
hear them? even see him-
self as the punches land?

Bill says "we must descend" but
which way down—the roads are
both south and west, a great store-
house of furs, weaponry, and descent I
would
          stretch my
voice
                    with the wolves in the
middle of Superior

                         but other

waters
          own
                    me

in Springfield's Levee, not a
river but "a kind of history
taking place" in Cansler's
Tavern, the oxtail soup and
the Gruesome Five warming
up

     "it's not the music, but
the sense of displacement"—
the riots in 1908, a George
Richardson "outraged" a
Mabel Hallam by his skin
and the rioters stole guns
from Fishman's, cut fire
hoses as 40 homes burned;
William Donnegan (married
to a white woman for thirty
years), his throat slashed,
then hung in a tree—refugees
housed at the Armory; 5000
Guardsmen walking the streets—
postcards from lynching photos,
"what happens to Negroes in
this town"

                 the kids scream
out in black and white, hurling
jujubes at the screen of the
Pantheon   "we waited 'til
after the cartoons"   then a
1 A.M. cheeseburger over the
black and white tiled Jack
Robinson System (clearly not
"The Georgian")   and Hank
Jones saying to Kenny Barton,
"What are you doing in *this*
town?" and the women upstairs
that she never trusted

                         ("in a
few cases they attempted
retaliation"

rust and scab—Chicago's heel,
the nation begins here—ponds
channeling fire, spores exploding
from flash towers on the city's
southwest side; every residue of
the process, every lung devoured

not some "bright guilty place,"
but in headlights, an owl rising
from the ditch; the next, moon
over an ammoniaed, deadened
prairie

      postwar barbed wire
pushing against cornfields and
fence posts eyelidding a dormant,
corporate insomnia; navigation by
Mars

      (the beauties of speculation

"what's the price of your land,
buddy?"   call a panic or
recycle the debt—hedge against
a barrio gunshot or a crack blown
in the levee—put it all under
"eminent domain"

RANDOLPH & FIELD   O,
the mold's insistent embrace
of the concrete—*it makes me
hot!*—its respirations against
these caves, their hard, secret
histories of curtain and frost—"an
architecture of impermanence"
split open and ailing with light,
like the stone buildings were
pulled up out of the lake, cement
still sweating glaciers; is that a
church bell or nostalgia for six
o'clock ringing against western
sky, now petrified over the

CONGRESS HOTEL

the city encrusts itself on the eye—
not "limestone in its communion
with water," but urban caves, an
architecture made of dusk, glass
reflecting the city's shadow and
inside, bemused molds and the
weedy stink of summer—"a
common Mediterranean fantasy
of stone and water"

song of the mold:
we are the mold—
the infected archive,
encrusted underpass,
the summer city the
breath in your lungs,
the crawlspace song

do you sing to us, you
in your shrink-wrapped
homes, your goggles and
numbered viruses, chlorine
suits and flying machines?
in Flagstaff and Amarillo,
Oklahoma City and Gallup?
from your tinted windows
and sea to shining sea, do
you hear us, singing to
you as we eat time?

"they asked me how I knew"
what was planted in us—

mold exists in memory;
everything in reverse—
animals inside things,
piloting the Chevrolet,
the reptile in my heart—
your uncomplicated smile
as we chased the goat
through the building

a drifting, middling
civilization, addicted to
bottom lines—what
roads does *it* build?

(this is the yr of Jackie

Chevrolet skin covering the men's
threats—crack open the radio and
history's dust-stung residue bleeds
into the middle night   or peel the
men's sweat back over their muscles
cramped over seats

the Chevy is a cave
the Underworld turns
around these men their
eyes make sterile numbers;
Joe McCarney turns his straw
hat in the green night

                        their eyes
full of blood, they've seen
closed things—what they
believe about the country
could fit into a paper sack
or a concrete wall   they
see future wars, their eyes make
not bloated animals but string
corpses along a cigar store
calendar

        "roaming the freeways
for half the night—where else
would they go to rehearse the
end of history—the meaning of
freeways, they'd always known"

                the fist in time—
we've got the Italians in the car—
prairie Venice, the streets running
with river water, lower Randolph, a
great cave of history   the mold
swallows you

16

your passenger is asleep whistling
some tune between snoring   "is that
Dixie?" you ask   in America,
you travel alone great birds appear
along the weedy edge, violence
crouching in the spilled headlight 2
hrs. outside Chicago and you want to
wake him but—
                        too late now   passing
Wilmington and Bainbridge   still an
hr. to the all-night fill-up at Bloomington,
Springfield by sunrise, work by nine

"blood in its peaceful rage"

for the middleweight championship of the world

Zale ruled the first four rounds—
Graziano's right eye opened, then
closed by punches, his brow seeping
blood—Zale knocked Rocky down
in the third, but Graziano (155 lbs.)
stunned & hurrying to his feet

on home turf, Zale made $150,000 from
          the gate plus 40% of the $30,000
radio rights; Graziano, the New Yorker,
          claimed about $75,000 plus 20%

the butcher's song:
"you talk about your prevenient grace"

history

                used to be
about
    something

now
it's about
pop rocks
& blowjobs

the prophecy
            of
                    Chevrolets

I've got Milton
Friedman in my
head—"corruption is
government
                    intrusion
in the
form of
        regulation"

and you
moving along Sixth
Street,
            glass display cases
flying
                in your wake

        *(one hundred miles from Chicago and the map's no
goddamned good*

look, friend (he
expld) it's not
like I'm trying to
screw your wife
or anything—I
just need you to tell
me how to get west
          and you keep
sending me to Joliet;
if I'd wanted to go
south, I'd 've gone to
Cairo   to Memphis
to Jackson   to New
Orleans

he sd, America
is a road is a broken
chair is a jail cell is a
fault line

a corruptible geography
pre-Cambrian plates over
a fucking river that won't
stay in place   roads
stretched over fault lines

"nothing in writing
          is easier
than to raise
                the dead"

a history of cockfighting in Chicago?
you might as well write a history of
the molds growing in the locker rooms
of Chicago Stadium—

                    "this is pleasure"

a phenomenology of violence has to be
told in pieces, scratches of narrative—a
tale pieced and told by a butcher

                              "every-
thing was dust and panic"

                    the Springfield
butcher and the pharmacist from Kankakee (it
sounds like a joke, right?)   one day, a guy
sours, corruption eats him—the whole planet
covered in a layer of mold, sometimes 2000
feet thick—but how they *knew* the city, *de-
scended* into it—the landmarks along Halsted,
Ogden, crossing West or South Side—who or
what's waiting there for you, carrying a dead
man's knife in your pocket?

(get your kicks. . .

the clack of the break at
Capitol Billiards—men in
long chairs, cues balanced
against bent knees—"free
and easy," and the constant
awareness of men observed
as they measure the angles,
count the balls left on the
table

      whether the fighter
is ever aware of such opened
space: the shots he's taken,
the first sign of blood, spit
bucket placed at his feet—the
ring's geography, Graziano
coiled in the sixth

           or if the
land is aware of itself, its flat-
ness stretching south by west—
*Oklahoma City looks mighty
pretty*—and how do you be-
gin to imagine San Berna-
dino? the Chevy accelerates
the slow curve, extending night

(the ring shot from the rafters)

"we enter regions of coherence
and of settled forms"

                       the highway
slab—the boxing ring—light
descending through smoke and
heat, the fighters' bodies uncoil
in sinewy forms   *life is
grotesque when we catch it in
quick perceptions—at full vent,
history shaping itself*

                    (RD 6) *how
do you beat a jabber?* the Chicago
fight unfolded in a series of four
Graziano rights—the first, a flash
of muscle and cover, and the second,
a slick fist moving more than just air
(Joe McCarney fans himself with his
straw hat)   the third opened a cauldron
of blood and Zale saw the fourth as a
black glove—the crowd erupts, figures
painted in smoke, a moment quickened
in the referee's eyes—or *to be quick-
sanded by the fungus pulp of Hades'
purple hair*—Zale's brain explodes;
(did consciousness leave him or was
he merely overtaken by some other
animal? like the road, a crack opened
in land or time)   Zale fell backward
into a neutral corner, then forward
into the ropes (timekeeper Joe Lipp
counted, "one, two") referee Behr
called it there

                    the third fight
was in Jersey because Graziano had
failed to report three attempted six-
figure fixes to the New York State
Athletic Commission—and "the rest
was geography, all space and light
and shadow and unspeakable

hanging heat"

                    that July afternoon
at Chicago's Wrigley Field, Phillies' pitcher
Robin Roberts (known for his deft control)
hit Phil Cavarretta and Andy Pafko (both in
the back) with the bases loaded in the bottom
of the ninth to force in the winning run

                 (Cubs 3, Phillies 2

"a kind of history taking place"

the map, coffee spilt and corrupted—
not by the mapmakers, who put made-
up towns in Louisiana and Kansas
to protect their copyrights—but by
the compass itself; to go west, you
must go south—*we must descend*—
Bill knew it—corruption finds its own
level, like water; try cutting the weather
out of the land—mold sealed in the
walls, the prairie spreads by fire

the prosecutor's song:
I'll show you my hyena tattoo if
you demand it—what we have
here is not the soft money of re-
bate and donation but the hard
dollar of kickback and patronage,
nepotism and ham-handed bribe;
the pocket stuffed green—pure
corruption, power stuffed for a
death on a tropical beach—this
is corruption, pure and simple,
and it must stop here, my friends

Bill says "we must descend" and
the road runs south to Springfield,
but downward? descent to the
river or Route 66 ascending west,
the nation dreaming with it—rail-
roads and underground rivers and
embattlements and the big, easy
commerce of men exchanging hands—
"To fail without fail: this is a sign
of passivity" this is not Mississippi,
or is it?— he eases the throttle and
the Chevy moves downward into
prairie, into rivers, into Illinois

>   *how do you map this?*

America is a great cave
turned above ground its spaces
light   animals run the walls
carved by headlight, the men
take all this in without words

your eye catches fenceline your head
leaks distance   the Mercury in
front of you gathers hitchers, deposits
them on streetcorners in Wilmington
and Joliet

do we corrupt the land
or does it corrupt us?

          (the blood not corrupted, but prairied

does the memory ever
bleed? (not *why* but *how*
we must descend)

stunned to an eight-count
the gash   the opened eye
the body blow   the con-
tusion   punches numbered
and scaled   rounds scored

history leaves no such measured
numbers, although it leaves blood

corruption blooms in the blood—
"from the stink of the diddy to the
              stench of the shroud"   (he'd
heard that one

corruption takes space (haustoria
breaking down cell walls,
puncturing their soft,
porous
integrity and
leaving a softer death)
not stones, but weeds and molds

in their
silent
taking of

land

"the powdery mildews
grow superficially on the
surface of the host"

black mold—canker and
wilt   rot blight and mildew
leaf spot and rust   scab
and smut *as agents of decay*

                    history is
asexual—some dead echo
of ourselves, an infection,
an underworld, underskin
          (the men traveling
know this)

                    "invasion
occurs commonly by in-
halation or through small
wounds made by splinters
or thorns; although deep
infections are not common,
they are sometimes fatal"

song of the mold:
do we swallow the past
or does the past emerge
from us?

we've been grocered and
pharmacied, brokered and
rackjobbed ("the true begin-
nings of nothing but the
Supermarket")—

          measure our
velocities, keep us under-
ground, unexposed, withheld
in bits, like taking death out
for an afternoon walk   we
will sing through you, your
hands, voiceboxes, and
Chevrolets

see how he belongs to the cutting
block, to the wallow of trembling
muscle and mess

                              does the butcher
shape or chop, his hands do violence
or sculpt? define the carcass's form or
dissolve its anatomy? the animal's
body coming apart, like the boxer's
in jabs and hooks—doing as much
violence to himself as the man
circling him?

                    likewise, how does
the geography leave its print on the
land? does it define or segment, give
names or sever names from their places?
a national road should name things

            (where does that road go, tell
me—California or Texas?

                                    "a
sense of birthright and usable history"
our voices are not stand-ins for his'
try but are cut from the rock of time
itself—*a certain meaning to these*
eviscerated beasts

(the mold exists in human evolutionary memory

she screamed, *snake!* and
it was your job to get the
knife from a white shed-
ful of blades   not a
machete, more or less
rusted down to a digger,
metal poked into ground—
something to get at the
weeds along a lake home's
sidewalk

                    laying out the
reptiles, the backyard fungi—
a snake's mouth is not an
oracle, it moves among stems,
caps and stones—your eye
lingers on the blade

you'd always believed that
you were headed west, under-
stood that the Luddites had
joyless sex; you could claim
an authorized future—this is
Eden, right?

capped in the ditch, a
plastic milk jug, three-
quarters full of blood,
beside the coke cans,
popsicle sticks, and
inevitable insects—
the land's revenge on
us, eating up every
petty larceny and
grand misdemeanor—
the road moves tiredly
through the land (35
seconds to dissemble
each hog); it numbers
and drains, it runs from
the Porkopolis and
bleeds the River dry

violence or a nostalgia
for violence? not video
gore or the sorority girl's
shriek, but the order of it—a
corpse in a Missouri corn-
field, the body in a Texas
car trunk, the stiff right
uppercut

                    "the last
scalp taken in the West"

the hand located in the
foundation, the electric
chair at Statesville, bullets
plucked from a West Side
apartment doorframe

*on all, the voice of mold falls,
present, loud & sure*

and the men retreated into desert
(even here the mold blooms)
drawing equations on chalk
boards, on notebook covers,
on cave walls, on the backs of
other men's wives

these sexless
nymphs   under a
sexless moon, cradled,
          atop the

          ALLERTON HOTEL

     (*that mule kicks*

"in them
          the dark glow
of the mold was

          everywhere"

these men
had to keep
reminding them-
selves that they
believed in
history

they kept the
governor's head
in a box, dis-
played it inter-
mittently in rest
stop men's rooms;
they kept dollar bills
in shoeboxes, the
country in a post
office box or an
off-color joke

"there's a dead
man in the entry-
way of America"

ring management, or the
measure of an opponent's
vulnerability, his circling
feet scraping canvass; his
movement now stirred
against air plasmic with
crowd, one-thousand degree
floodlights and smoke
rising from underground

not violence
but nostalgia—
pressed into
hands, their
navigation of
the road back
tunneling south
into the land, a
pasture conse-
crated by blood

the Mother Road not
"cut into the land" but
swallowing descent—
"the odors of wood,
flowers, and decay
that one smells with
extraordinary pleasure
for a few yards before
emerging from a cave"

a southwest Missouri
picnic stop, a New
Mexico gas station
lighted at one A.M.,
the butcher behind
his counter in a very
public space, central
Illinois farmhouse:
BREAKFAST 24 HRS—
Joe McCarney chewing
his bacon across from you
"the marathon of
danced-out plots"

you've mapped them;
nostalgia takes you into
the ground (i.e., Spring-
field's Levee district
as nostalgia)
                        to the
ladies and gentlemen
of the jury, corruption
is only an artifact—
stacked shoeboxes of
one-dollar bills, an eleven
o'clock plane ticket to
Buenos Aires or head-
lights pursuing Fred
MacMurray down a
dark road, roostertails
following ("you can talk
about your sin"); spores
explode from toxic silt—

but what sad, relentless
explosions?

"a canal is not a ditch,"
he sd, walking the bridges—
                overnight,
it'd become a city of ugli-
ness he could not recognize,
not even when a woman
pulled a gun on him on one
of the quays that separated
the city from its shadow

(the road between Springfield and Chicago)

"it's not the music—
it's the sense of
displacement"

governing not by prose or verse
but by geography   those white
spaces
        in the map   "the endless
tuck and fold

                of politics"

                                George Ryan,
Kankakee

                pharmacist, Governor

                        of Illinois

the indictments began Dec 2003 (convicted Apr 2006),
Justice Dept Prosecutor Patrick Fitzgerald's assertions:
18 counts of patronage and favors,
levels of corruption, Ryan's administration
"a low-watermark for public service"

        against that, the law school hall (11 Jan 2003)
and Ryan's commutation of 157 death sentences
(among his last acts as governor)—
names unraveling like prairie spaces*

(dead presidential words)

        the governor sd,

                "mercy bears more fruit than strict justice"

---

* United States District Judge Rebecca Pallmeyer barred all mentions of
Ryan's death penalty position from the courtroom during his corruption
trial. Ryan had placed a moratorium on the death penalty in Illinois on
31 January 2000, citing 13 cases where individuals had been
wrongfully convicted and given death sentences since 1977.

the reporter's song:
would the governor take the
stand in his own defense?

                         over
his shoulder, he chats up the
press:

          How are Ozzie and the
boys on the South Side playing
this week? What happened to
the hitting? You can't live on
homers, you know

                    (notebooks in hand,
we laugh)
                    but the question, governor,
it must be asked:

          do you have any regrets?

the governor's song:
I would speak in my own defense
the courtroom is myth-filled I've
never known a gun I've built two
highways for the gods and a third
is promised

          "the mold invaded
my childhood by consuming an
untended orchard next to my home—
trees and fruit devoured by bitter rot,
black rot, blossom end rot, canker,
rust, powdery mildew, rubbery wood
and scab—mushrooms of all colors
sprouted under diseased branches—
masses of ink-caps bled the grass"

I was schooled in mold—every
pharmacist is;

          "because I had suddenly
seen that the world was held together
only by frost and by freezing, by con-
traction, that its bowels contained huge
compressors and ice-cold molds—a
trivial Indiana landscape"

imagine America as a
collection of edges: the
Mother Road, the light
marking one fighter's
space, a truck stop's rack-
jobbed Paydays, mold
against a tree branch

"understanding the history
here is like looking up a
goat's ass," he sd (he tried
to explain it all to me,
tracing the life cycle of a
dissolving Eden on a paper
napkin) we always mistake
rust for mold—not oxidation,
but the sweet science of
seepage, a slow seismic flood;
waters'll retake the land—you
cut yourself and the infestation
begins—maybe that's why
you draw the blade against
your own pantleg as you
approach the snake—not
waves of enzymes, but a
gentle dissection, haustoria
pressing membrane—the
snake moves through ivy
before the knife

song of the mold:
"Tight houses are the problem"
not a defect of nature, but faulty
construction, inadequate flashing
and leaky pipes, one hundred-
year floods—the house is unclean
and the priest will do what priests
do

                          or where there's
a leprous disease in the fabric—
warp or woof of linen or wool—
"the great mixing box of his'try
will sound" and "he who eats in
the house shall wash his clothes"

                          the stone is
sick   why try to resist some
part of yourself, for "he shall
break down the house, its stones
and timber and all the plaster
of the house; and he shall carry
them forth out of the city to an
unclean place"

Nixon sd, "this is a
nation of laws" but
see *decades of bad
lawyering*

Nixon's
four (Rehnquist, Powell,
Blackmun, and Berger)
dissenting in *Furman v.
Georgia*—see *keeping
the vote down* and *can
we construct a system?*

and June 1972, Lester
Maddox on the courthouse
steps: "it's a dark day in this
country—rape, murder, and
anarchy—reentry to the
jungle life"

eye for an
eye "embedded in the
American psyche"

MUFFIN KOTE® *is a specially formulated dusting compound— effectively protecting the muffins against surface mold growth. It produces a dry, nonsticky dough surface to facilitate transfer as well as an attractive texture on the muffin.*

the governor's song:
"and I liked the way history
did not run loose here—
segregated and visible—they
caged it, funded and bronzed
it—enshrined it carefully in
museums and plazas and
memorial parks—

                        the rest
was geography—all space
and light and shadow and
unspeakable hanging heat"

all that heat packed away, a
spinning microgeography, its
spin mimcs an America—

*the car on the road
the town on the map
the highway into the distance*

town being "an expression of
security and confidence—
the human terrain there—"

now you buy the best advice,
ask to be pointed west, but
it's always goddamned south;
the compass is busted; every-
thing spins circles: the boxer in
his ring, the cytoplasm streaming,
the spinning arm—it's "circle up
the wagons, boys"

                        *the melancholy
and relief of knowing we shall soon
give up any thought of knowing
and understanding the conquered
cities—the desperate moment
when we discover that this empire
is an endless formless ruin, that
corruption's gangrene has spread*

too far to be healed by one
scepter

		and all we have is
the spindly courts; justice
sitting on his dead pecker
bench   "this is somebody's
America"

the judge's song:
let me remind you of the facts of this case—
"The hog eats the corn, and Europe eats the
Hog. Corn thus becomes incarnate; for what
is a hog, but fifteen or twenty bushels of corn
on four legs?"

                    But here, we're no Cincinnati;
our town is the end of line where death has
taken a new shape—we no longer depend on
the seasons, what grows on or under the earth—
no adhesive death frightens us, the deathwheels
spin comfortably in our homes and heads, we
convert these animals into commercial pork.

this man denies all this sacred machinery—
the dissembly line, the railroad economy,
the trade in shadows; he slaps a price on high-
ways, music, and invention—maybe he thinks
he owns the future, that "we all grope towards
Persephone's fate"—but we are here to remind
him that "geography has moved inward and
smallward"

                    we've trapped shadows here:
in the testimony of witnesses, in the incompletion
of complicated plots, in the underhistory of us all—
there! there's no mold on my breath, no vulture-
shit on my robe's fringe or docket, no weeds
growing between my knees

                    I jab the air—
you can take these pigs to market—*there,*
you son of a bitch; how do you like that?

the governor's song:
what's more
what's
what's
what's more
more
more American
what's more American
what's more American than
more
more American
than screwing
than
what's more American
than
what's more
what's more American
than screwing
than
than
than screwing
what's more American than
the landlady
what's more
more than
than screwing
what's more American than screwing
what's more American
more American than
what's more American than screwing
what's more American than screwing the landlady
the landlady
what's more American than screwing
screwing the landlady
what's more
more
what's more American than screwing
the landlady
for
what's more American
what's more American than screwing the landlady
for
for

for rent
what's more American than screwing the landlady
what's more American than
than more
than
what's more American than screwing the landlady
the landlady
for rent
what's more
what's more American
what's more American than screwing the landlady
for
screwing the landlady for
more
what's more American
more American than
the landlady
what's more American than screwing the landlady for rent
for rent
for rent

"turn up the radio—I like
this tune"   the nostalgia
of the three men in a Chevy
is never private; there's always
the matter of the road—gray,
striped, and public—moving
into the country, descending
among ditches

                to fall in love
with such a tune (never public);
the news comes on the radio—
the velocity of a murmur
passing through the land,
faster than a shout, than
your velocity, fixed but
intent, small movements
furtive and stealthy
exiting the car;
                your posture
of disbelief and
threat—hands on
hips, moving along
the polished rail,
the glass flying in
your wake

        the cut
of a
cop on
  pension

        (*you hated lawyers*

days of rage

        days of butchery

                days of illness

mold
for
        days

the governor's song:
I know what you're thinking—
men in suits do violence—perhaps
you've had some violence done
to you; you're asking, "where's
your suit, old man?" I keep it
here, in my trunk—besides, what's
more poetic than *getting things
done for people*
                    "So I'm here,
am I? a crowd of starlings waddle
over the crusted snow of last year's
seeds—like those sterile instruments
whose appetite is operation—but I
was no one's son—spores in air begot
me—cocked, I look through you"

you can write your *History
of Cockfighting in Chicago*
(write it in the dust) but it isn't
going to exhaust the game,
(this man was always
talking)   Fuck you,
I explnd—what's more
Chicago than a room of
screaming men, stirred
up by blood whether
it's between their knuckles,
or in their eyes?—you'd
drive 200 miles to see it—
Bullshit, he sd—nobody's
gonna buy that, my friend, a
roomful of screaming men,
of fighting chickens, of
blood   a new dark age
blooms only once a lifetime

not a sick mouth but
sick lungs   the dust
there incomprehensible
to him

the butcher's song:
I never wore cartoon or coverall,
traced stem to soil, or slipped
my hands into the empire's soft
cement—instead, toeing the spores
raised by last night's rain and
listening for news from the plaza,
I kept my revolts to the backyard—
the shined-up slide slick with bird-
shit—I could dismember a bird in
my sleep, open its body to the
preacher's mouth—reclined in
the Sunday violence done to
outbuildings   the newspaper
was my song, "the tale of the
tape"—the men moved about the
ring on curled toes, looking for
a space to slide a punch

you stand here, bag of
salted popcorn in hand,
afraid of
            speaking too much
into the past or too much pro-
tein in the blood

we watched the games
from the car through chain-
link fence—who needed to
see the batter anyway? you
had a name for every umpire
in the Association and
taught them all to me

insulin and sugarless 7-Up's
in the fridge, death's con-
stellation in your lungs your
skin an angry wrapping some
-thing sick-skinned something
half-eaten, chicken in grease-
sopped cardboard your t-shirt
torn in the flank, a mad
red heart drawn on your
chest—red ink on cotton

song of the mold:
you have to understand this—
some things don't know corruption;
we adapt to your fruits and concrete,
inhabit every corner of the empire,
the waters bent there—

                    we move
within and against these things,
natural

          as bees sailing
                         the Dan Ryan,
the waters
          ditched and guttered
                         there

"the moisture sucked from the
joints and foundations"

the governor's song:
it's no longer a question of
shoeboxed one-dollar bills, but
if it please the court, there're
questions that must be asked:

have you ever been booked?
have you ever ridden on the
state's money? or had Wm.
McKinley sign your check?

"when they took him away,
one sat beside him, the other
rode backward because the
state's money has a face to
each backside, and they are
riding on the state's money,
which is incest"

                    map that,
you Osage geographers!

the bonfire rots soil
in its own time—
woodshed the color
of birdshit and each
kicked-open toadstool
a threat

        or the Chicken
Industry in America—each
bird skinned and cooled,
plasticked and shelved

    ("the cumulative violence done to birds in this land"

the governor's song:
eating light, I emerge from the ground—
I hardly recognize my own son, my
legacy is corruption

                        I've forgotten
more names than I know, the backshelf
pharmaceuticals, the things given with a
wink—was that the Illinois Central or a
tornado?

                        I descend in a Kankakee
minute; you get homesick for the mold,
but who are the prosecutors of the
world? every childhood has its recalled
storm, its horse's nightmare eye, the
run to the cellar (sadly, most of ours be-
long to Dorothy—the hired hands racing
the black cloud, the witch turning on her
bicycle)   the prairie can't hold it—

the leaf mold on courthouse steps
the shredding of paper
the ripple of rising water
the ignition switched off and
the car running down into midnight

"it's
like America," he
sd "all out
on bets"

ANOTHER ACT OF RANDOM VIOLENCE

open the wide, confused country-side;

   recover the "habits of spot"

the foreman's song:
"it's the new corruption"—he
explained it for the ladies and
gentlemen of the jury—one
day, a guy sours & corruption
eats him

          corruption leaves
no landmarks, just a silence
in the land—again, new
words like *felons* & *criminal*
and "violence is a residue"

the governor tried—he sd
"Abraham Lincoln was a
helluva guy" although we'd
heard that confession before,
the habits of obedience, the
sovereignty of power—"he
was a man of the West"
                    (that explains it)

the prosecutor sang, "ideas
used to come from below—
now they're everywhere above
you, connecting things and
grids universally" they fed
us the muffins wired for
sound, then we cheered
the smoke, the metal,
& the bullshit

corruption has its own
intelligence like a fist
knows its face, a virus
its host

      it's a cultural
memory, right? going
into the Converse Tavern
at age six, buying a Miller
High Life for you

                    or
driving I-55 from Chicago
in the cramped ass-end of
a Volkswagen, cold prairie
flying against glass

                   I
go looking for traces of
swamp along buildings—
gray sickly dog piss smells,
signs of carbon breakdown,
a great fire's slag pushed
into the lake—mold is a
chemical process

the governor's song:
I was scared of my home place.
I feared it.
I lay down to sleep with my clothes on.

"the instigation to invasion is apparent:
ready profit—

              the excuse also is apparent:
progress"

              I rearrange these stones
for Anthony Porter and William Donnegan,
for Gary Gauger and Lawrence Hayes, for
those at Parchman Prison

                          but ever the druggist,
I traffic not in stones, but in weeds and molds; I
am a pharmacist who had the good fortune to be
elected governor of this great state, my duty
to study the sequence of punishment "cruel and
unusual and freakish in its imposition"

                          540
executions in the United States between 1991
and 2000 (152 in Texas alone under W)

"I never thought of a last meal"
          (the history I emerged from

no sweet science, no
Theogenes; against ropes,
no-name Midwest pugs
slogging at the Armory,
Lanphier Ballpark (flag
waving in the middle of
centerfield) or the
Fairgrounds

but savage fights—
spit bucket and a chin
for prairie, fists packed
with night—"pull off
pieces of themselves
to form the fat of the
new bounty;

                    the half
logic of stealing from
this immense profusion"—
this nostalgia takes you
into the ground; in the
gravel, a reluctant piss
flicked like a switch

they asked me how I knew,
my true love was true

songs on the Levee

(what fucking river?

the governor's song:
corruption in the capitol murmur
corruption in the weights & measures
corruption in the headlights
corruption in the blood supply
corruption in the memory
corruption in the river
corruption in the map
corruption in the legislature
corruption in the prosecutor's eye
corruption in the beans
corruption in the campaign ledgers
corruption in the facade
corruption in the butcher block
corruption in the road
corruption in the rulebook
corruption in the foot
corruption in the radio voice
corruption in the docket
corruption in the tax code
corruption in the henhouse
corruption in the cleaver
corruption in the mouth
corruption in the gray matter
corruption in the food supply
corruption in the witness box
corruption in the cell
corruption in the judge's gut
corruption in the game
corruption in the feed
corruption in the reservoir
corruption in the currency
corruption in the chicken itself
corruption in the prosecutor's throat
corruption in the ring
corruption in the foot
corruption in the map
corruption in the press corps
corruption in the eye
corruption in the song

the bailiff's song:
America is not some giant,
psychotropic green pepper
for your investigation; who
is the third-rate confidence
man now? some fourth-rate
Don Juan unzipped—rain-
making or muckraking, it's
all the same to me—I take
my cuffing slowly—let's be
reasonable, surrender your-
self to me an arm at a time to
their metal clickings against
mold and rust—I'm only a
machine of justice, *death
and magic, that's the mush-
room!* I cleaned the butcher
block with a diluted bleach
concoction—together, we crave
filling and eagerly grab for
what there is; corruption's
geography takes you precisely
where you want to go

"gonna buy that man a pair of
cement Jordans" brightly tied
against night—remember us,
standing outside the Stadium,
hands in pockets, cold as hell,
waiting to watch Air himself
pour in forty points against
Detroit, wag a finger at Isiah

        (you never saw Jordan

this wasn't your game—despite the
Armoried city tourney, you preferred
Lew Alcindor to Kareem, found the
blues a corruption of whatever tune
sounded in your head, that car, its
green radio light blaring Cash and
twang

        the game was your way of drawing
a line against the screaming Midwest gyms;
rooms of men and blood were preferable—
some sweet science—long drives into night,
escaping north

                but America itself preferred
roomfuls of that blood, not a corruption but a
fulfillment of every document, every descent
into the land

                the gyms hollered
with descent, every point shaved, every
hard pick and ticky tack foul—every referee
a bagman for the empire, governors of sweet,
sweet spoil

        *(the governor's shoes
stare up at me
        from his desk—
bronzed,
                they bloom with dried flowers*

water runs toward earth
as corruption runs toward
blood and ink (spores
explode into sky) not the
same bacteria, but ancient
colonies deathwheeled
into necropoli, recycled
cities on the plains (no
roads between them)

"step into the ground and
see what blooms there"

the old man
doesn't trust
the spellings
of words,
complains that
no one knows
things' names,
least of all,
this kid

hellbox
imagination
homesick
for grandma's
kitchen
cabinet
junkshop
all-night
Tarzan flicks

between his
fingers,
the eraser

*Do you follow
cleverly devised
myths?*

        just my own

Dear Sir—your
slack jaw has been
colonized as have
your kidney, tongue
and metacarpals   leaving

you with sore hands
and a sick mouth

your city has been colonized
your face has been colonized
your eye, too   spores
drifting across air and concrete
their song stinging time

try to
make a
history

          book

out
          of
     this

the body is
quick
          as a fault line
opening it-

          self to the
violence thrown, de-
scending

to caves

          to canvass

                    to dogs deep

in the earth
                    (the shoulder
          's a fulcrum; it snarls
gently, its joint unfolds in the
punch delivered then

                              taken—the counterpunch

          working with the
mouth

          ZALE'S A DEATH MACHINE

did you see his fucken hands?!

big as ping pong paddles,
fingers bent and clenched like
a black and white photo

the memory

          hopelessly

corrupt

what is mold's memory?

paint a mural in the dust—
the song sounds like
moving water or
stinking onions

"this history is on the air"
gray with spores, green
with age   *do we matter?*

a kind of materiality
our blackness is our song

    "decay is temporary"

I fold my memory into
smaller things—cheeked
snarl   bonefire   my feet
in blood grass   self-coat
hung on a widow's hook;
time smells like piss

NOTES ON THE VOICINGS OF SONGS
IN *HOSTILE WITNESS*

The songs of Hostile Witness include the voicings of Italo Calvino's Invisible Cities (New York: Harvest, 1978), William Cronon's Nature's Metropolis (New York: Norton, 1991), Don DeLillo's Underworld (New York: Scribner, 1997), Clayton Eshleman's Juniper Fuse (Middletown: Wesleyan, 2003), William Gass' The Tunnel (Normal: Dalkey Archive, 1999), Michel Houellebecq's The Possibility of an Island (Gavin Bowd trans.; New York: Vintage, 2007), Nicholas Money's Mr. Bloomfield's Orchard (Oxford: Oxford, 2002), Thom Jones' The Pugilist at Rest (London: Back Bay, 1993), and the web site of Archer Daniels Midland.

On former Governor George Ryan's hard questions to the death penalty process in Illinois, see Deadline (film directed by Katy Chevigny and Kirsten Johnson, 2004).

Made in the USA

SPARK PLUG ATTITUDE

Igniting the Spark Within!

Never Underestimate
THE POWER OF ATTITUDE!

Anthony B. Thomas

with Jacqueline Thomas

Copyright © 1999 by Spark Plug Publishing

All rights reserved. No part of this book may be reproduced, stored in retrieval systems or transmitted in any form, by any means, including mechanical, electronic, photocopying, recording or otherwise without prior written permission of the publisher.

Printed in the United States of America.

This book is available at a special discount when ordered in bulk quantities.

ISBN: 0-7392-0124-7
Library of Congress Catalog Card Number: 99-93060

Printed in the USA by

3212 East Highway 30 • Kearney, NE 68847 • 1-800-650-7888